THE HOUSE
THE CARPENTER BUILT

Additional copies may be ordered from the publisher for educational, business, promotional or premium use.
For information, contact ALIVE Book Publishing at:
alivebookpublishing.com

Book design by Alex P. Johnson

ISBN 13
978-1-63132-242-6 Paperback
978-1-63132-250-1 Hardcover
978-1-63132-241-9 Audiobook
978-1-63132-249-5 Ebook

Library of Congress Control Number 2025931685
Library of Congress Cataloging-in-Publication Data
is available upon request.

First Edition

Published in the United States of America by ALIVE Book Publishing
an imprint of Advanced Publishing LLC
3200 A Danville Blvd., Suite 204, Alamo, California 94507
alivebookpublishing.com

PRINTED IN THE UNITED STATES OF AMERICA

10 9 8 7 6 5 4 3 2 1

THE HOUSE
THE CARPENTER BUILT

An allegory of the greatest love story
ever designed with you in mind

Kathryn Mignani

ABOOKS
Alive Book Publishing

This book is dedicated to you, the reader. After you read the section entitled, "How This Book was Built," you will understand it is not accidental that these pages were published. I have no doubt the plan from the beginning was designed specifically with you in mind.

Contents

Foreword

Among the many allegorical works that literary history has yielded, from the early pens of Langland and Bunyan to the works of C.S. Lewis, there exists among these a subset genre that sees the soul through the metaphor of a house. Most famous of these would include Teresa of Avila's *The Interior Castle* (1588) and more recently, Robert Boyd Munger's beloved *My Heart, Christ's Home* (1954). Into this tradition, Kathryn Mignani brings a fresh offering with her delightful *The House the Carpenter Built*.

The allegory of "soul as house" is intuitively rich and accessible to a broad and diverse audience, as most people spend a significant portion of their lives inside various dwellings. The metaphor yields ideas of home, safety, explored and unexplored areas, quality and disrepair, building and expansion, threat and danger, identity, aesthetics, location in the world, and much more. Having these ideas seamlessly move between the physical and the spiritual is immediately intuitive and highly instructive for those who have thought little about spiritual realities.

Mignani's straightforward and simple allegory is a gift offered to those who would like an introduction to spiritual themes without being addled or harassed by religion-peddlers. In particular, *The House the Carpenter Built* reintroduces Christianity to audiences that have either grown indifferent to its thrilling message due to the inoculation of over-exposure and dulling familiarity or that have grown antagonistic to its gracious message due to misrepresentation by either clumsy or mean-spirited handlers.

Mignani's treatment of the Christian story is marked by gentleness and grace, even as she does not shy away from its hard-edged truths. Still, it does so consistently within the perspective of the generosity and love that undergirds what the church, through the ages, has lovingly called "the gospel," an old Greek word that translates as "good news," the very thing this new work makes tangible to the reader.

I have known Kate for many years and know that she writes from a place of authentic spiritual transformation grounded in the soil of suffering, perseverance, a deep love for God, and life-long generosity to the friends and family that surround her.

Welcome, then, into the warm and hospitable space of Kate's imagination. Sit down in the living room of her soul-house here under construction on the pages that follow, take a warm cup of coffee into your hands, breathe in deeply, look around with a touch of curiosity, and find yourself at home.

– Dr. Jeff Reed

Note From the Publisher

Having worked in the publishing industry for more than twenty years, one thing I have come to understand is that people have many different reasons for writing books. For many, it is their preferred artistic expression—it's just "in them" to express themselves through the written word. These are the novelists—the storytellers—who build castles in their minds and craft wonderful stories about the castle-dwellers, hoping to spell-bind the imaginations of eager readers.

For others, it is a quest for the brass ring of commercial and financial success. Their writing is a form of barter, offering to solve problems, meet needs, or render advice in exchange for a few dollars. If their ideas are groundbreaking, they may even have the makings of a new career—*if* those few dollars evolve into a steady stream over months and possibly years.

Still others are merely people who have experienced life in ways they believe to be unique or challenging. They feel compelled to help others navigate the life-altering hurdles they successfully cleared. Their reward is found in knowing their suffering was not in vain.

And then there is another type of author. This is the person who does not set out to write a book. They are called to a higher purpose—a *divine* purpose—that they neither sought nor dreamed about. The ambition to "be" a writer wasn't even on their bucket list.

I can count on one hand the number of authors who

might fall into this final category among the several hundred I have worked with over the years. These are individuals who have not so much as written a book; they more likely *transcribed* it as delivered to their heart and subconscious from on high.

Kathryn Mignani is one of those in this select category. I knew this immediately upon reading the original manuscript of the book you now hold in your hands. I also knew this perfectly composed construction manual *needed to be published*.

This is not to say that Kate lacks anything as a writer. She does not. But when I read this the first time, I reacted in a way that I cannot express in words. Suffice it to say that tears of joy were involved as Kate's tale about this carpenter and His work rang true. This wasn't just another book; it was, in my judgment at least, *inspired art*.

And so, I will only say that *The House the Carpenter Built* was not written solely by Kate. She had some extraordinary help assembling words that may touch the deeper reaches of your soul—*if* you are open and willing to allow Kate and her "helper" to guide you there.

—*Eric Johnson, Publisher*

Meeting the Carpenter

As I looked around my house, I realized that I had let it fall into disrepair. And not only the house but the land around it. How had I let it get like this and how had I not noticed until now? I felt discouraged and embarrassed. I also felt lost not knowing what to do or even where to begin. A feeling of hopelessness started to creep in.

It was at that moment that a carpenter I'd heard of approached me and asked if I would like him to rebuild my home. His offer was the beginning of a wonderful, challenging, exciting, frustrating, and mysterious relationship.

The conversation he started continues to this day. It started when I accepted his invitation:

Sam: Of course, I would love to have my house rebuilt, but I don't even know where to begin. I am certain that I cannot do it myself. None of my previous attempts to improve my house have lasted. I've given up.

The Carpenter: You must have heard about the work I've done for other people. If you will trust me, I will rebuild your house if you let me handle the entire project.

Sam: You? You're only a carpenter. You are not a designer or architect. I want to talk to that person about my ideas for changes and upgrades.

The Carpenter: No, I will only do the work if the drawings are done by the Master Architect. I only follow His designs.

Sam: I've heard of him but have never seen him. He's supposed to be good but does he know what my place needs? I hear he lives far away and he seems a bit eccentric, if he even exists. From what I've heard, his price is more than I can pay.

The Carpenter: I can assure you, it will be a custom design tailored specifically for your needs and desires. I will work something out with the Master Architect if you are willing to cooperate with me.

Sam: What do you mean by "cooperate"?

The Carpenter: The plans must be followed exactly with no shortcuts. I only do top-quality work. All work must be done with permits and approved by inspections. I have an owner's manual that you need to study as well.

Sam: Okay, let's say you get the Master Architect to re-design the house for me—what happens first?

The Carpenter: I need a permit to do the job. You need to decide if you are willing to agree to the terms and sign the contract. Once you've done that, I will have the authority to proceed.

Sam: So the bottom-line question is: Do I trust you?

The Carpenter: Do you?

Sam: I think so. Enough, at least, to get started.

The Carpenter: That's enough for now.

Work Begins

THE DEMOLITION CREW SHOWS UP

Sam: Why are you taking down these walls?

The Carpenter: So we can build the right kind of walls.

Sam: What's wrong with these?

The Carpenter: They were poorly designed and built. These are walls for a fortress, not a home. These walls were designed to keep you inside and others out. The front door is surrounded by a solid brick wall. The only way to see out is through a small peephole that distorts your view of those outside. This is a dark place. The new door and walls will be constructed to protect you while new windows will allow you to see the outside clearly, letting light in.

Sam: I'm afraid to let these walls come down. Where will I go? Won't it be dangerous for me to stay here?

The Carpenter: While there is risk involved, I will never leave the project. I will protect you during the reconstruction. Not every wall that you've built is defective. I will only dismantle the ones that need to come down.

THE EXPOSED FOUNDATION HAS CRACKS

Sam: When do the new walls go up?

The Carpenter: After we lay a new foundation.

Sam: What? What's wrong with this foundation? It only has a few cracks.

The Carpenter: The cracks are enough to cause your new home to shift in certain conditions. This foundation was built on sand. We need to go down to bedrock and replace this foundation with a rock-solid one.

Sam: Won't that take a long time?

The Carpenter: It will require patience on your part. This is a good time to study your owner's manual and remember the promises that are in our contract.

Framing and More!

THE FRAMING HAS BEGUN

Sam: Wow! The new frame is up already! I was expecting to see a new foundation not a framed-out house.

The Carpenter: It's amazing how quickly you can build on the right foundation.

Sam: I wouldn't have thought it possible.

The Carpenter: The possibilities are endless. Take a look around the worksite and give me your impression.

Sam: I see wood cut to various lengths to fit perfectly into place. I see reinforcements of different types, and everything seems quite orderly.

The Carpenter: "What does that tell you about your new home?"

Sam: Details matter.

The Carpenter: That will be very important to remember.

VENTILATION & PLUMBING WORK IN PROGRESS

Sam: What's going on here? There are trucks in my way and boxes and pipes strewn all over the place.

The Carpenter: You seem frustrated.

Sam: I deal with a lot of garbage all day and now I come home to a disaster area. You bet I'm frustrated!

The Carpenter: The ventilation and plumbing are well underway.

Sam: And what exactly will this accomplish?

The Carpenter: You will now have appropriate outlets for steam and waste.

Sam: I guess I could use those . . .

The Carpenter: You will have a reliable source of pure water.

Sam: I'm glad you're here.

Break Time

WORK STOPPAGE

Sam: What is going on? It looks like the work has come to a complete stop?

The Carpenter: It has.

Sam: Is there a shortage of materials or a problem with scheduling?

The Carpenter: No.

Sam: Then why has the work stopped? We are not even close to being finished.

The Carpenter: Today is a scheduled day of rest.

Sam: Rest?! So the project will be delayed by a whole day just to get rest?

The Carpenter: The project is not delayed. Rest is part of the plan. It is not "just" rest; it is "must" rest.

Sam: How many days are we resting?

The Carpenter: Just one for now.

Sam: For now? How often is this "must" rest going to happen?

The Carpenter: Once a week.

Sam: Every week? That is going to set our timeline way back.

The Carpenter: Quite the opposite. The plan is to work wisely instead of foolishly.

Sam: I don't understand.

The Carpenter: Have you heard of the law of diminishing returns?

Sam: Oh yeah. The principle that there will be a proportionally smaller gain as more energy is invested.

The Carpenter: That's right.

Sam: I feel guilty not working when I know there is so much to be done.

The Carpenter: Pehaps it will help to think of it this way: leisure is a luxury afforded to royalty. Perpetual work is the lot of slaves. Which would you rather be?

Sam: Royalty.

The Carpenter: Then there's no place for guilt on your day of rest.

Sam: Okay! I find reading relaxing. Any suggestions for a good book?

The Carpenter: Yes, I know an excellent one. It's a best seller.

Back to Work

SIDING, ROOFING & GUTTERS GO UP

Sam: Wow, such progress! This looks great! I can see the materials that went into these are top quality.

The Carpenter: They will provide solid protection from the elements that will batter your home.

Sam: Don't you mean "might" batter my home?

The Carpenter: No. Make no mistake, storms will come but you do not need to fear them.

Sam: You're sure I will be protected even when gale winds blow and torrential rains come?

The Carpenter: Yes. The storms will come, but you will be in a safe refuge.

Sam: So, regardless of what hits my home, I will be protected?

The Carpenter: Yes. Remember we started with a rock-solid foundation. Every facet of the building process has been designed with your safety in mind, so you can be at peace regardless of the circumstances that surround you.

THE HOUSE GETS REWIRED

Sam: What are all these wires for?

The Carpenter: You need new wiring in this house.

Sam: We can't reuse the old wire? What a waste.

The Carpenter: Remember the permit? Your new wiring needs to meet code; the old wire didn't. The old wires were unsafe and the connections corrupted.

Sam: What could you possibly do with all this wire?

The Carpenter: Your new wiring will bring in light and power, as well as provide a flawless communication system. All connections need to be clear.

Sam: This goes back to the "details matter" discussion, doesn't it?

The Carpenter: I'm glad we're clear.

INSULATION, DRYWALL & PAINT

Sam: After seeing what all the wiring accomplishes, it almost seems a shame to cover it up.

The Carpenter: You can be assured its effectiveness does not depend on being visible. Insulation is another protective measure in the Master Architect's plan for your home. What do you think about your new walls?

Sam: They create individual spaces, yet there is a natural flow between rooms that seems to invite movement. The house now seems open and welcoming.

The Carpenter: Good observation.

Sam: The colors add such beauty. The design is clearly by a true artist. I could never have asked, thought, or imagined that I would have such a beautiful home. It is amazing when I think of all the things that were wrong with my house and how I allowed it to fall into such dismal disrepair. Looking at it now, you would never even know all those imperfections were there in the first place.

The Carpenter: Funny, I don't remember the imperfections at all . . .

FLOORS GO DOWN

Sam: I can't believe the floors have been laid and floor coverings installed. Why are there different kinds in different parts of the house?

The Carpenter: Each kind serves a different purpose.

Sam: "The carpet is really soft; I like this room. This will be my retreat.

The Carpenter: I'm pleased to hear that. This room was designed to provide comfort. It's an easy room to pass by but a very important part of your house.

Sam: Will you visit me here?

The Carpenter: I will meet you here as frequently as you wish.

Sam: Why did you use the flooring that's in the entryway?

The Carpenter: A lot of dirt and mud from the outside world will be tracked in through the front door. The floor's surface has been treated so the filth will not penetrate it. You must remember to tend to it whenever it gets dirty.

Sam: What about this floor? It seems very durable.

The Carpenter: It needs to be.

Sam: Oh, because a lot of foot traffic will go through this part of the house?

The Carpenter: Yes. People will walk all over it.

Sam: Are you sure it's strong enough to withstand the pressure over time?

The Carpenter: I am positive. It has been custom made to protect against the scuffs, scratches, and even trampling caused by people.

Sam: In that case, maybe I'll throw a party for my

neighbors, friends, and family to see what you've done here.

The Carpenter: Good idea. I believe they will be amazed at the changes since we started.

The House is Built and Beyond

Sam: I can't believe this is my house! It is fully functional and at the same time warm and welcoming. The Master Architect sure knows what he is doing. You never told me how you convinced him to design this project. I haven't received a bill, and I'm certain I can't afford to pay the price of such detailed and intricate plans. The cost must be exorbitant for a transformation that encompasses every part of my home. Is there some sort of payment plan?

The Carpenter: It's already been paid for.

Sam: Who paid my bill?

The Carpenter: I did.

Sam: You did? But why? How? When?

The Carpenter: Part of the Master Architect's master plan is to rebuild all houses that have fallen into disrepair, which is all houses but one.

Sam: Whose house is that?

The Carpenter: Mine.

Sam: Where is your house?

The Carpenter: I gave it up and it has since been demolished.

Sam: What?! Why? I don't understand.

The Carpenter: Long ago, the Master Architect designed and built the perfect house and gave it to me. You see, the Master Architect is my father and he trained me to be a skilled carpenter to work under his authority to convert dilapidated dwellings into custom homes. In order to partner with my father, I had to give up my house to be able to complete the rebuilding work I was called to do, and it was the only price the Master Architect would accept to rebuild yours.

Sam: So, you're saying that you gave up a perfect house so I could have one designed by the Master Architect. That's hard to believe.

The Carpenter: Not everyone who hears my story believes. The question is, do you?

Sam: Well, let's say I believe. If it is true, there is no way I can repay you.

The Carpenter: That's true. However, I am not looking for payment. This is my gift to you.

Sam: Gift?! But why? I've never done anything to deserve this.

The Carpenter: That's also true.

Sam: I've never heard of this kind of extreme generosity. Why on earth would you do such a thing?

The Carpenter: For heaven's sake, I couldn't stand by and watch your old house deteriorate with you inside!

Sam: It certainly would have been condemned; you really saved me.

The Carpenter: That was the plan.

Sam: I have a crazy idea. Since you gave up your house, will you come and live in mine?

The Carpenter: I was hoping you'd ask.

Sam: Is that a "yes"?

The Carpenter: Yes. I happily accept your invitation. You understand that I will need to continue working here.

Sam: Working? But it's all done. Everything is great. No more work is needed.

The Carpenter: For the moment. Believe it or not, shortly there will be scuff marks, scratches, and dirt on your freshly painted walls. Fresh paint will cover the imperfections. In time, light bulbs will burn out and furniture will need to be replaced.

Sam: How will I know when and where more work needs to be done?

The Carpenter: Do not let your heart be troubled. I have already provided for a caretaker to advise you each step of the way. In fact, he's been here from the first moment you made the decision to trust me.

Sam: The whole time? But I've never seen him. Are you sure he's here?

The Carpenter: Yes, although he stays out of sight, the caretaker is intimately familiar with the Master Architect's plan for your home and will direct you accordingly. Remember the communication system that went in? With a still, small voice, he will remind you of the hard work that has already taken place and will encourage you to read your owner's manual for clear direction moving forward. The warranties in the manual are there to give you peace of mind. You will want to commit those to memory.

Sam: Is there anything else?

The Carpenter: "The caretaker will remind you to rest and will counsel you to allow repairs and home-improvement projects. You can trust his direction as my own and proceed with confidence.

Sam: It's that easy?

The Carpenter: It's that simple, but it will not be easy.

Sam: But you'll do the work, won't you?

The Carpenter: Yes, but remember I will need a permit for certain jobs. And I need your continued cooperation.

Sam: I thought when the re-building was complete I'd be finished with this process. Are you telling me that I'm going to spend the rest of my life working on it?

The Carpenter: Yes, but never alone. I have seen the plans and know that someday it will be complete. I can already picture your beautiful, finished home.

Sam: You can?

The Carpenter: Yes; it is absolutely perfect.

The Master Architect's Invitation

If you want to follow the amazing plan designed especially for your life, the Master Architect of all creation invites you to join Him on the exciting and fulfilling adventure that awaits. It is as simple as humbly accepting His invitation. Although you will face challenges in the ensuing improvement process of your life, you will never face them alone. The caretaker of your soul will gently guide you in truth and love. Simply pray these words:

> *God, I believe You are the Master Architect who sent His Son to pay the price with His life so I would be set free from all condemnation for eternity. I acknowledge my need for a savior and welcome You into my life. Help me to cooperate in completing the divine plan You have for me as I walk each day in gratitude for what You have done. Amen.*

If you accepted the invitation by reciting the above prayer, know that you are a very specific answer to my prayer! Now, find a faith community that adheres to Biblical principles and teaching, where you can engage and be supported and encouraged. I look forward to meeting you, whether here or in eternity.

I BELIEVE

We all have the opportunity to build meaningful and fulfilling lives regardless of the changing circumstances around us. The key is to have a firm foundation on which to build and to accept each phase with humility and gratitude, pursuing truth and engaging in healthy community.

Building Plans

Just as it requires planning to remodel our homes, improvement in our lives also takes intentionality, and there is value in evaluating your current condition before pondering next steps in building your dream home. Toward that end, the following pages are provided to aid you in assessing your present state and in developing a blueprint for next steps. The great news is—regardless of your current life phase— **if you are still breathing, you are a beautiful work in progress!**

Evaluation of Current Conditions

Foundation: (the base(s) upon which you rely for stability*)*

_____

_____

Framing: (your physical features, size, shape, characteristics)

_____

_____

Temperament: (your character, nature, how you respond to the circumstances around you)

_____

_____

Priority Determination: (how you decide what to allow into your life and what to keep out)

_____

_____

Safeguards: (how you protect your inner self from harmful outside influences)

_____

_____

Communication Methods/Style: (your motives and conduct in expressing yourself to others)

_____

_____

Emotional Regulation (how you respond to heated situations and being treated coolly by others)

_____

_____

Boundaries: (welcoming appropriate relationship while ensuring proper times of respite and protecting against unhealthy influences)

_____

_____

Caretaking: (that upon which you rely for direction/decision-making moving forward)

_____

_____

REMODEL CHECKLIST

Foundation
Underpinning upon which your life is built

Framing
Physical features: size, shape, and layout for designed purpose

Ventilation
System ensuring appropriate temperament regardless of outside environment

Plumbing
Method to bring in what is clean and dispose of what is not

Siding, Roofing & Gutters
Safeguards to protect the interior from various outside elements

Wiring
Clear communication channels

Insulation, Drywall & Paint
Safeguarding warmth in cold times, cooling in hot times with a steady and attractive surface

Flooring
Appropriate areas to welcome guests, provide respite, protect against permanent stains

Caretaking
Reliable maintenance plan to ensure proper care on an ongoing basis.

FOUNDATION
(Underpinning upon which your life is built)

Current condition: _____

Goal condition: _____

Steps I can take toward achieving the goal:

_____

_____

_____

People/other resources that can help me in the process:

_____

_____

_____

My first step will be:

_____

_____

FRAMING

(Physical features: size, shape, and layout for designed purpose)

Current condition: _____

Goal condition: _____

Steps I can take toward achieving the goal:

_____

_____

_____

People/other resources that can help me in the process:

_____

_____

_____

My first step will be:

_____

_____

VENTILATION

(System ensuring appropriate temperament regardless of the outside environment)

Current condition: _____

Goal condition: _____

Steps I can take toward achieving the goal:

_____

_____

_____

People/other resources that can help me in the process:

_____

_____

_____

My first step will be:

_____

_____

PLUMBING

(Method to bring in what is clean and dispose of what is not)

Current condition: _____

Goal condition: _____

Steps I can take toward achieving the goal:

_____

_____

_____

People/other resources that can help me in the process:

_____

_____

_____

My first step will be:

_____

_____

SIDING, ROOFING & GUTTERS

(Safeguards to protect the interior from various outside elements)

Current condition: _____

Goal condition: _____

Steps I can take toward achieving the goal:

_____

_____

_____

People/other resources that can help me in the process:

_____

_____

_____

My first step will be:

_____

_____

WIRING

(Clear communication channels)

Current condition: _____

Goal condition: _____

Steps I can take toward achieving the goal:

_____

_____

_____

People/other resources that can help me in the process:

_____

_____

_____

My first step will be:

_____

_____

INSULATION, DRYWALL& PAINT
(Safeguarding warmth in cold times, cooling in hot times with a steady and attractive surface)

Current condition: _____

Goal condition: _____

Steps I can take toward achieving the goal:

_____

_____

_____

People/other resources that can help me in the process:

_____

_____

_____

My first step will be:

_____

_____

FLOORING

(Appropriate areas to welcome guests, provide respite, protect against permanent stains)

Current condition: _____

Goal condition: _____

Steps I can take toward achieving the goal:

_____

_____

_____

People/other resources that can help me in the process:

_____

_____

_____

My first step will be:

_____

_____

CARETAKING

(A reliable maintenance plan that ensures proper care on an ongoing basis)

Current condition: _____

Goal condition: _____

Steps I can take toward achieving the goal:

_____

_____

_____

People/other resources that can help me in the process:

_____

_____

_____

My first step will be:

_____

_____

Acknowledgments

I genuinely believe this book only came to fruition due to the contributions of many, some of whom are acknowledged by name below.

My Grandfather: Otha Clark Crawford. Heartbroken to lose him while I was still a little girl, I remain thankful for the years I lived with him and my grandmother until I was eight. Although not a church-goer, he prayed the "Now I lay me down to sleep" prayer with me bedside each night. I am certain this is the reason I came to believe there is a Master Architect. I still miss you, Grandfather.

The Weller Family: It is still curious to me how a neighborhood family came to invite the new girl in their son Jim's third-grade class to Sunday School back in 1969. I had never been to church and did not know what Sunday School was. (It is also curious to me that my mom would let me go with strangers.) Who knew Jim and I would end up as lab partners in a high school chemistry class! Thank you Weller family—that Sunday changed my life and eternity.

"The Lady in the Big Group": How I wish I knew her name so I could thank her properly here. Thank you for sharing the message that is retold here in allegory form. That day in Sunday School brought untold relief to my little-girl heart, one that worried constantly about being "good enough" to go to Heaven. Even at eight—and a good girl— I knew I could always be better.

Carrie O'Ban of Cherry Lane (at least in 1969): The teenage Sunday School teacher at Walnut Creek Presbyterian Church who took me seriously when I said I wanted to ask Jesus into my heart after hearing the message in the big group. I do not know if I spelled your name correctly or where you are 50+ years later, but I want to honor you as the one who prayed me into new life.

Diane Camp: My former teaching leader at BSF who graciously agreed to read and comment on the 2002 draft of the book. The final draft incorporates many of her suggestions. I will always be grateful for your teaching and for your kindness to me.

Dr. Jeff Reed: Former senior pastor at Hillside Covenant Church, published poet/author, and dear friend. Jeff is the one from whom I learned that rest was a luxury of royalty in Biblical times. His teaching re-famed my view of Sabbath. He is also the one who presided over my remarriage, agreeing to incorporate many quotes from a shared favorite movie, *The Princess Bride,* which he did masterfully without the guests being any the wiser. Jeff, I am a better person because of your teaching, friendship, and humor. Let me know what you think of this published work. Remember, this is for posterity so be honest.

Susan Reed: A dear friend (to whom Jeff is married) and is the godliest woman I have ever known—a humble beauty with a servant's heart. Soos, I miss our reservoir walks and will forever treasure the daily encouraging texts you sent when I was in the darkest season of my life, even when I didn't have the strength to reply. Even though we now live in different states, I carry you in my heart and look forward to a time when we can catch up in person.

Michele Miller: M2: Truly one of the most amazing people I have ever known. I think your title is "Program and Facility Manager" but it should be "Miracle Worker"

("Michele, let's build a mountain!"). You were there for me when I needed to find a way to pay bills and skillfully organized all my paperwork while I wept with my head on the table and then years later when you catered our wedding reception. Truly a friend of the hills and the valleys!

Ginny Kaminitz: My BFF. From "Baby's 1st Christmas" to today when those babies now have babies, you have been a treasured friend. Your kindness, generosity, and humor ("skittles!") have encouraged me through the highs and lows. You are the one who taught me the "double recompense" principle and that scars can be beautiful (goodness knows you and I have our share of those). Glad we are on this path together and that Gerald and Russ have joined us.

Joy and Randy Fischback: Precious (and fun!) friends who have done more for me and my family over the years than I could ever detail here. So many treasured memories. You were my go-to the day my world fell apart and welcomed me with open arms, cancelling plans and making me a grilled cheese sandwich. You'll never know how much that meant to me. I realize I will never be able to thank you enough or repay you for all your kindness but hope this acknowledgment brings you some of the honor you deserve.

Judith and Kevin Gabie: My heroes on multiple levels. Kevin, your dedication as Riley's youth leader and direction when the locks needed to be changed strengthened and encouraged us in a difficult time. Honored to be co-cub scout leader with you that one year with those "fire-breathing chickens!" Judith, you are one of the most courageous people I know. Your willingness to share vulnerably and boldly is only matched by your gentleness and grace. I wish we lived closer.

Karen Trestrail: A friend closer than a sister and second mom to my oldest daughter. Karen, from the first day of kindergarten when Ashley and Kelly met, you have been a beloved part of our lives. I don't know how I would have made it through those parenting years without you! Your loyalty and ability to love sacrificially are rare qualities. I treasure our coffee dates with the girls and how you faithfully plan and host them. Thank you for being my dear friend, Ashley's second mom, and Mina's Auntie Karen.

Brian Gleason: Former youth pastor, friend, and beloved officiant at my daughter Kelsey's wedding. You provided valuable guidance when our home became unsafe during the summer of 2011 and came to the immediate rescue when Brody needed a secure place on that fateful day in October – with video console and games in hand!

Eric and Peggy Johnson: New friends brought together in a community group. Eric and Peggy, I am still amused that God plopped you both in our living room after I told Him years earlier that I had no interest in seeking out a book publisher. Classic Him. I so appreciate your willingness to read the manuscript and am grateful that you published it. I am most thankful, however, for your friendship, and I am excited that your dream—Red Geranium Project—is coming true, too!

My Children

Ashley Makowsky: My oldest who is truly an old soul. Ash Kash, I so admire your commitment to truth even when it's hard. Thank you for always being the "family glue." Your devotion to our family and the intentionality you bring to it unquestionably shaped the close-knit dynamic we enjoy today. Grateful Michael embraced our family as his own (he takes the best pictures!) and that the two of you gave us Mina Kathryn!

Kelsey Moore: My younger daughter with a competitive yet sensitive spirit, a truly beautiful combination. Kelsey My Belle, you are genuinely one of the smartest people I know, and I so admire your persevering work ethic while maintaining a healthy work/life balance. You and David are good reminders to me that humor and gathering just for fun make life better. Thankful for the love and extraordinary quick wit he brings to our family!

Riley Smith: My oldest son, intelligent, resilient and tender-hearted. Ri, I've watched as you endured so much loss early in life. You weathered the storms in a way that yielded a soft heart instead of a hardened one. I do not know of any other teenager whose only birthday wish was to raise enough money to return to serve the people of Haiti. Please know you continue to make me proud. Lindsay is a beautiful addition to our family, purposefully planning opportunities to get us together. You and your bride make a good team!

Brody Smith: My six-foot, seven-inch Professional Engineer "baby" with an adventurous spirit. Brod-Man, your life mission statement declared at the age of eight, "I'd rather have fun than be safe," has certainly been a theme to date. I admire your courage in taking risks and committing to the follow through they demand. As your chosen path has led you geographically away from the rest of our family, thank you for continuing to make all of us priorities in your life. Your regular calls bring me more joy than you know.

Russ Mignani: My incredible husband. Love, thank you for pursuing and persevering when I did not want to be pursued. Your unconditional love is exemplary of our Lord's. Over the past 10 years, I have observed your kindness to all, extending grace even to those who do not recognize or appreciate it. Thank you for encouraging me to publish this book. Grateful to be on this journey with you (and you're still the cutest boy I've ever known!) I cannot express the degree to which your loyalty to me and care for my family has brought healing and hope back into my life. Beauty for ashes for sure.

Marlene Clark: My "surrogate mom," now in heaven. I miss you every day and am weeping as I type this. I hope you are the one who greets me when I get to the other side. Thank you for loving me sacrificially in so many ways and taking me to coffee every Wednesday morning during bar prep, asking me questions. I still think of your reaction to the legal meaning of "mayhem" whenever I hear the word! I am convinced you are a big reason I passed the bar on the first try.

The Last Shall Be First: Of course, the most important acknowledgement goes to The Master Architect, The Carpenter, and The Caretaker. Quite literally, there are not enough words to fully express my gratitude to You, the three-in-one. With deepest appreciation, I offer this small book—in the same manner as the boy who shared his small lunch over 2,000 years ago—to nourish all who would receive it. May it bring You glory.

How this Book was Built

What started as a personal creative-writing endeavor in 2002, *The House The Carpenter Built* has now become a published work. Not surprisingly, during the interim two decades, I experienced the various "building" stages depicted in the book. Although a simple story typed on few pages, I pondered the possibility of sharing it some day, even as a published piece.

Over the past 23 years, that very thought would periodically surface.

As life would have it, I lost those few pages in the midst of raising four children, going through a heart-shattering divorce, moving to a small fixer-upper, going back to school, and getting re-married. Although they were lost, I never forgot about those pages or the possibility that they could be shared some day.

Periodically, I would tell God that if He wanted me to do anything with the draft, He would have to help me find it first. As His specialty is finding the lost, I was not surprised when I found it within the past year.

I have also told God more than once that I was not necessarily interested in being a published author, and I definitely was not comfortable promoting a short story to a publisher, so if He wanted it published, He would need to pave the way.

Enter Eric and Peggy Johnson.

The Johnsons joined a short-term community group we hosted in the sping of 2023. Instant connection. They continued attending various short-term groups we hosted and we quickly became friends. It was during one of these later groups that I learned they are—you guessed it—*book publishers*. In the moment, I secretly looked heavenward and silently said, "Are you kidding me?!" Book publishers literally delivered to my doorstep.

Even I recognized this as a sign. However, I was not comfortable asking my new friends to publish the story. Next conversation with God. (By now, you know where this is going…)

In the spring of this year, we did a seven-week video series entitled *Transfomations* (Rick Warren). Each week, we learned about the importance of health in various areas of our lives. After watching a video and discussing the week's health topic, we were to set a related goal to accomplish within three months. Some goals take extra courage . . .

One of my goals was to review my initial draft, update it, and garner the courage to ask Eric and Peggy to review it. Goal set. What was not set was the time to achieve it, so spring turned to summer. Then, an unexpected block of time suddenly surfaced, as did the motivation to re-type the original story (yes, the old Word Perfect version lives on an old computer somewhere).

Next came the hard part: getting enough nerve to ask Eric and Peggy if they would read it. One Sunday morning, with heart pounding, I handed the copy to Eric, explaining my goal to "finish and submit" my story. He graciously took the pages and said, "It has been submitted" and promised to read it that afternoon. In a same-day text message, he said, "It must be published."

Over dinner the following week, we discussed next steps, including the suggestion to expand one of the topics (about the Caretaker) and other ideas, one of which was to include this very segment: how this book was built.

I hope this story about the story will encourage you to patiently persevere in whatever is being built in *your* life.

About the Author

"Kate" is a joyful work-in-progress, grateful for each phase in the unfolding blueprint for her life. She is the proud mother of four amazing adult children, mother-in-law to three wonderful additions to the family, adoring Mimi to granddaughter Mina & grandson Lewis, and wife to Russ, who keeps her laughing and well fed, something to which his own seven adult children can attest. He is also Papa to five grandchildren for whom Kate gets to be Nonnie. Great-grandson Daxtyn was welcomed in April of 2025.

Kate holds a bachelor's degree in Political Economy of Industrial Societies from the University of California at Berkeley. She previously had a career in communications then transitioned to her role as stay-a-home mom of four children (her favorite job). She returned to the academic setting in her mid-50s, obtaining a paralegal certificate and subsequently attending law school at night for four years while working fulltime as a paralegal. At the age of 58, Kate graduated first in her class at John F. Kennedy College of Law. Since July 2020, she has practiced civil and family law.

Currently, Kate works full-time as a family law attorney

in Walnut Creek, California, where it is her privilege to walk alongside hurting people during the same dark season she experienced previously, reassuring them there are brighter days ahead. She was named a Rising Star by Super Lawyers of Northern California and is a member of the Christian Legal Society,

When afforded the opportunity, she enjoys hearing people's life stories over a cup of black coffee and a slice of pumpkin bread, escaping to the mountains of northern California, or shopping at Hobby Lobby.

In line with her life mission statement – to serve as a witness of God's faithfulness, particularly to the discouraged, through communication, encouragement, and laughter — Kate's deep desire is for all who read this book to know how deeply loved they are, each a unique masterpiece designed for honor and significance.

A portion of the proceeds
from the sale of this book support non-profits like

The Red Geranium Project
(scan code to visit RedGeranium.org and learn more)

ABOOKS

ALIVE Book Publishing and ALIVE Publishing Group
are imprints of Advanced Publishing LLC,
3200 A Danville Blvd., Suite 204, Alamo, California 94507

Telephone: 925.837.7303
alivebookpublishing.com

www.ingramcontent.com/pod-product-compliance
Lightning Source LLC
Chambersburg PA
CBHW041924090426
42741CB00020B/3478